YOU'D *never* BELIEVE IT BUT...
the Sun was the first clock
and other facts about time

© Aladdin Books Ltd 1999
Designed and produced by
Aladdin Books Ltd
28 Percy Street
London W1P 0LD

CLD 21583
This edition was published in 2000 for
Colour Library Direct Ltd,
New Mill
New Mill Lane
Witney
Oxon
OX8 5TF

Designed by
David West • Children's Book Design
Designer Flick Killerby
Computer Illustrations
Stephen Sweet (Simon Girling & Associates)
Project Editor Sally Hewitt
Editor Liz White
Picture Research Carlotta Cooper
and Brooks Krikler Research

ISBN 0-7496-3428-6

Printed in Singapore

A big thank you to Lizzie and Hattie for their wonderful drawings.

YOU'D *never* BELIEVE IT BUT...

the Sun was the

first clock

and other

facts about

time

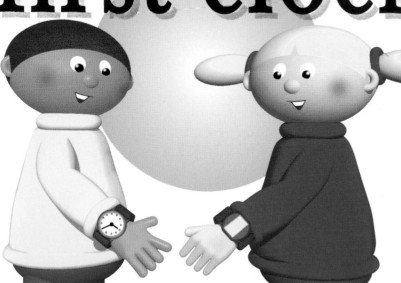

Helen Taylor

Colour Library Direct

Contents

Introduction

You can see clocks and watches everywhere; we use them to tell the time. You even have your own body clock which tells you when it is time to eat or sleep. But did you know that people used to tell the time by looking at the Sun or by melting candles?

Join Jack and Jo as they discover some fantastic facts about time.

FUN PROJECTS

Wherever you see this sign, it means there is a project which you can do.

Each project will help you to understand more about the subject. You'd never believe it but... each project is fun to do, as well.

Time for everything

There is usually a special time for the things we do every day. Do the people in your house often say things like: "Hurry up, it's time for school!" "Is it lunch time yet?" "What time does my television programme start?" When do you need to know what time it is?

What's the time?

We use clocks and watches to tell the time. You can see them everywhere.

Time to get up!

The Sun seems to move across the sky. It rises in the east and sets in the west. The Sun is higher in the sky in summer than in winter.

You'd never believe it but...

The Sun was the first clock. People used to tell the time by the position of the Sun. When the Sun is at its highest, it is 12 o'clock mid day.

MAKING A CLOCK
You will need a paper plate, a butterfly clip, a long hand and a short hand cut out of card. Write the numbers 1 to 12 around the edge of the plate. Ask an adult to push the butterfly clip through the hands and the middle of the plate. Now you can move the hands around to make different times.

Day and night

Daytime begins when the Sun rises in the morning and ends when it sets in the evening. Night-time begins at sunset and ends at sunrise. Most people work during the day when it is light and sleep at night when it is dark.

> It's daytime on my side of the world.

The Earth travels around the Sun, spinning on its axis as it goes. It takes 24 hours to turn once on its axis. We call this a day. As the Earth turns, half of the Earth is facing the Sun and is in daylight. The other half is facing away from the Sun and it is night-time there.

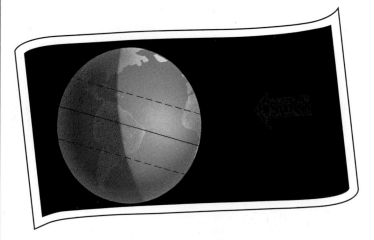

PICTURE DIARY
Draw a timeline like this showing the different times of the day. Then write in or draw a picture of something you might be doing at each time of day that is shown.

It's night-time where I am.

Venus

You'd never believe it but...
A day on Venus takes 243 Earth days, it spins so slowly. A day on Earth takes 24 hours.

Telling the time

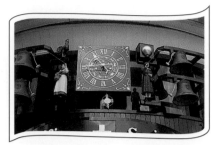

When we tell the time we use hours, minutes and seconds. There are 24 hours in one day, 60 minutes in one hour and 60 seconds in one minute. It takes one hour for the long hand to go all the way around the clock.

Our watches are showing the same time.

Some clocks have a hand that shows the passing seconds. It takes one minute for the second hand to go all the way around the clock.

A digital clock shows the time in numbers. The first two tell you the hours and the second two numbers tell you the minutes. On some watches another two show the seconds.

You'd never believe it but...

A second is a very small length of time, but it can be split into parts of a second. Sprinters have to be timed in hundredths of a second to be sure who has won a race.

But they look very different.

KEEPING A RECORD

With a friend, find out the answers to these questions. How many hours do you sleep at night? How many minutes does it take for you to eat your lunch? How long is your favourite television programme? How many seconds does it take for you to write your name? Do you both have the same answers?

Keeping time

People have been using simple clocks to tell the time for more than 3,000 years. The Sun makes a good simple clock by casting shadows on a sundial. A candle with notches can also be used to measure passing time. These clocks are not very accurate, however.

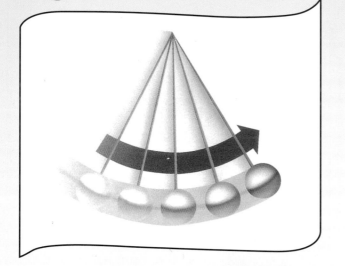

The scientist Galileo discovered that a pendulum always takes the same length of time to swing to and fro, no matter how much of a swing it is given or how heavy the weight is on the end. This makes it an accurate tool for keeping time.

MAKE YOUR OWN SUN CLOCK

Fix a pencil into a piece of clay. Stand it in the centre of a piece of card and place the card on a window sill that gets a lot of sunlight all day. Every hour, mark the shadow and time. Use the sun clock to tell the time on the next sunny day.

Most clocks and watches have cogs, springs and wheels inside them. These work together to make the hands go round.

You'd never believe it but...

Electronic watches contain a quartz crystal. The crystal vibrates when energy is passed through it. The vibrations activate a motor which moves the watch hands.

A year

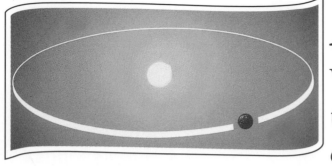

We use years, months and weeks to measure time longer than a day. It takes 365¼ days for the Earth to move around the Sun. We call this a year. Every four years there are 366 days in a year. This is because the four quarter days are put together to make an extra day. We call this a leap year. The extra day is 29th February.

I'm ready for the school outing.

Monday
Tuesday
Wednesday
Thursday
Friday
Saturday
Sunday

You'd never believe it but...

People who are born on 29th February only have a birthday once every four years.

The Moon takes 28 days to move around the Earth. We call this a lunar month. As it moves, the Moon seems to change shape depending on how much light from the Sun it is reflecting.

It's tomorrow. You didn't check the calendar!

A calendar shows you the days, weeks and months in one year. Do you know the names of the days of the week and the months of the year?

 USING A CALENDAR
Write important dates like your friends' parties or the first day of the school term on a calendar. This will help you remember them.

Growing up

All living animals are born, grow up and then become old before they die. Not everything takes the same time to grow. A year passes between each birthday and you become one year older. Every year you change and grow a little bit. You will stop growing taller when you are about 20, but you won't stop changing.

It's Tiggy's first birthday today.

Look at an old photo of you as a baby. How much have you changed?

You'd never believe it but...

Tortoises live to a very old age. A tortoise that belonged to the king of Tonga is said to have lived for 200 years.

> He's already grown up!

A BIRTHDAY BOOK

On your birthday, write how tall you are, your weight, draw round your hands and feet, take a photograph and put it all in a notebook. Keep it safe and do the same on the next birthday. See how much you have grown and changed in one year.

Plants have a life span too. Some live for only a few weeks, but there is a tree in the USA which is almost 5,000 years old.

Seasons

The Earth moves around the Sun, and it takes a year to go around once. The seasons change in some parts of the world as the Earth moves around the Sun. The places getting most heat and light are having summer, while other places are having winter.

It's too cold now for these summer clothes.

You'd never believe it but...

There are no seasons at all in forests near the Equator, the imaginary line around the middle of the Earth. It is hot and wet there all the year round.

PAINTING THE SEASON

Choose somewhere outside – in the garden, the playground or a park – and paint a picture of the scene. Put things in the picture, like clothes or the weather, which show what season it is.

In spring, the warmer weather begins. New plants start to grow, and baby animals are born.

Summer is the hottest time of year. Flowers bloom, and people often go on holiday in the sunshine.

I've found my favourite winter jumper!

Leaves start to die and fall from the trees in the autumn. It's a good time for picking fruit and berries.

It is sometimes snowy and icy cold in the winter. But when winter is over, it will be spring again.

Body clocks

You don't always need to look at a clock to tell the time. Your body has its own natural clocks that you can't see. Your pulse is a kind of natural clock that measures time between your heart beats. You can feel your pulse in your wrist and count how many times your heart beats in one minute.

It must be dinner time. My tummy's rumbling.

You'd never believe it but...

When you are asleep your pulse and your breathing slow down to give your body a rest.

Your body clock also lets you know when you need food and it is time to eat.

I know, I'm feeling really thirsty.

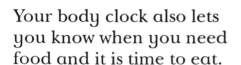

You also have a clock inside you that helps you to wake up in the morning and go to sleep at night. If you go on a long plane journey to a part of the world that has a different time of day, your body clock tells you that it is time for bed when everyone else is wide awake.

BODY CLOCK DIARY

Keep a diary of when you feel sleepy or hungry every day. After a week, have a look at it. Do you feel hungry or sleepy at roughly the same time every day?

Plants

Plants do not need calendars to tell them that spring is here. They can sense that the days are getting longer and that the air is warmer. A tulip bulb is buried underground in the cold winter. When spring comes, a new shoot pushes through the earth and the tulip starts to grow.

I can count 30 rings.

A tree keeps a record of the way it has grown. It adds an extra ring to its trunk every year. When a tree has been cut down you can count the rings in its trunk to find out how old it was.

You'd never believe it but...

You can read tree rings like a history book. A wide ring means there was plenty of rain that year. A narrow ring means the weather was dry.

This tree was the same age as dad is now!

Some plants, like a prayer plant, have natural clocks that seem to be able to tell the time of day. They open their leaves wide during the day but close them tightly at night.

PLANTING A BULB
Plant a tulip, hyacinth or daffodil bulb in a pot full of soil in the autumn. Put it in a dark place. Water it occasionally. In the spring, put it out in a warm, light place and watch it begin to grow.

Animals

Like plants, animals can sense when the seasons change from spring to summer, autumn and winter. These changes tell them it is time to behave in certain ways. Many animals have babies in the spring when the weather is warm and there is plenty to eat.

Caterpillars change into butterflies and moths in the spring and summer when flowers bloom and there is nectar to drink.

Look! The caterpillars are eating.

They will soon turn into butterflies.

You'd never believe it but...

It is summer all the year around for some birds. As soon as the cold winter weather begins, they fly to a part of the world where it is summer and there is plenty of food.

Hamsters and dormice get busy fattening up on seeds, nuts and berries in autumn. They go into a deep sleep, called hibernation, in the winter when there is not much food about. The fat they have put on gives them the energy they need while they are asleep.

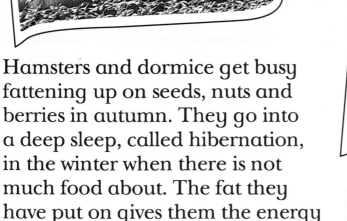

GARDEN CHART

Put some birdseed or bread crumbs out. Make a chart of all the birds you see that visit the food. Do this in winter and then again in summer. Is it the same type of birds that visit your food?

Fast or slow?

We use time to measure how fast something is going, or its speed. A car going fast takes less than a minute to travel a kilometre. You could time how long it takes you to walk a kilometre next time you go for a walk. It will take you a lot longer than a minute – you are much slower than a car!

I'm bored! Isn't it time to go home yet?

Sometimes time seems to go really slowly. When you are very busy or having a good time, it seems to go too quickly! Really, time always moves on at the same pace.

RACING TIME

Have some races with a friend. Who can write their name or get dressed the fastest? Use the second hand or a stop watch to time it and find out how long it takes to do each of these activities.

You'd never believe it but...

A cheetah is the fastest animal on Earth. It can run at 100 kph. Do you think a snail could even travel one km in an hour?

I'm having fun! It seems like I just started.

Long ago

The Earth is very old, and is changing all the time. New rocks are forming and old mountains are being worn away. Millions of years ago, the creatures and plants that lived and grew on Earth were very different from the ones alive today. We know about them because some remains have been trapped in rock and turned into fossils.

Layers of mud build up over the dead plants and creatures and press down on them. After a very long time, the mud and the remains of the plants and creatures turn into rock.

I've found a fossil!

Scientists use fossils to help them to work out the history of the Earth. You can find fossils in rocks or on beaches.

You'd never believe it but...

Dinosaurs died out millions of years before people first appeared on Earth.

It's nearly six million years old.

MAKING A FOSSIL
Choose an object like a shell or a leaf or even a plastic toy to fossilise. You will need: plaster of Paris, water, a yoghurt pot, a fossil object, plasticine, a teaspoon, a paper clip and some strips of card. Make a circle with the card and join the ends with paper clips. Press the object into some plasticine to make an imprint. Put the card circle around the imprint. In the yoghurt pot, mix the plaster of Paris with water, pour it into the circle and leave it to set. Peel away the plasticine and the card circle and you have a fossil!

Glossary

Axis

An imaginary straight line that runs through the centre of the Earth from the North Pole to the South Pole. The Earth spins around this axis.

Body clock

A natural clock that tells you when you need to eat, sleep or wake up.

Day

It takes the Earth 24 hours to turn all the way around once on its axis. We call this a day. Daytime is when the part of Earth you are on is facing the Sun and is in daylight.

Fossil

Fossils are formed when mud builds up over dead plants and creatures and presses down on them. Over millions of years, the mud and the remains of the creatures and plants turn into rock and become fossils.

Hibernation

As winter comes, it gets colder and food is difficult to find. Some animals have a body clock that tells them to sleep, or hibernate, until it's warm again.

Hour

There are 24 hours in one day. It takes one hour for the hour hand to move from one number to the next on a clock, or for the hour number to change on a digital clock.

Leap year

It takes 365 $\frac{1}{4}$ days for the Earth to go all the way around the Sun. Every four years the four quarter days are put together to make an extra day. We call the year with the extra day a leap year. A leap year has 366 days.

Minute

There are 60 minutes in one hour. It takes one hour for a minute hand to move all the way around a clock.

Month

There are 12 months in a year. All months have 30 or 31 days, except February, which has only 28 days and 29 every leap year. It takes the Moon 28 days to go around the Earth. We call this a lunar month.

Night

Night is the part of a day when the part of Earth you are on is facing away from the Sun and it is dark. Most people sleep at night-time.

Season

A season is a change in the pattern of the weather that brings changes to nature as the Earth moves around the Sun. Some parts of the world have four seasons – spring, summer, autumn and winter. Near the Equator, the imaginary line that runs around the middle of the Earth, there are no seasons at all.

Seconds

There are 60 seconds in a minute. A second is a small length of time. It takes one minute for the second hand to move all the way around a clock.

Week

There are seven days in a week. You usually go to school on Monday, Tuesday, Wednesday, Thursday and Friday. Saturday and Sunday are the weekend when you have a holiday from school.

Year

A year is the length of time it takes for the Earth to move all the way round the Sun. There are 365 days in a year.

Index

PHOTO CREDITS

Abbreviations: t-top, m-middle, b-bottom, r-right, l-left, c-center.

All the photography in this book is by Roger Vlitos except the following pages : 11t, 17t, 25t, & 26t — Frank Spooner Pictures; 13 & 29t — Pictor International; 16 — Flick Kilerby; 17b, 25m, 27mr, & 28 — Bruce Coleman; 18, 19all, 22m, 25b, & 27b — Spectrum Colour Library.